THE PROSPECTS OF MEDIEVAL HISTORY

AN INAUGURAL LECTURE DELIVERED AT CAMBRIDGE 17 OCTOBER 1944

BY

Z. N. BROOKE

Professor of Medieval History

CAMBRIDGE
AT THE UNIVERSITY PRESS
1944

CAMBRIDGE
UNIVERSITY PRESS

University Printing House, Cambridge CB2 8BS, United Kingdom

Published in the United States of America by Cambridge University Press, New York

Cambridge University Press is part of the University of Cambridge.

It furthers the University's mission by disseminating knowledge in the pursuit of education, learning and research at the highest international levels of excellence.

www.cambridge.org
Information on this title: www.cambridge.org/9781107698475

© Cambridge University Press 1944

This publication is in copyright. Subject to statutory exception and to the provisions of relevant collective licensing agreements, no reproduction of any part may take place without the written permission of Cambridge University Press.

First published 1944
Re-issued 2014

A catalogue record for this publication is available from the British Library

ISBN 978-1-107-69847-5 Paperback

Cambridge University Press has no responsibility for the persistence or accuracy of URLs for external or third-party internet websites referred to in this publication, and does not guarantee that any content on such websites is, or will remain, accurate or appropriate.

THE PROSPECTS OF
MEDIEVAL HISTORY

IT is customary in an Inaugural Lecture to render homage to one's predecessors, and it is a good custom to keep alive the memory of those whose labours are ended by reminding ourselves of what they did and what we owe to them. From this pleasant duty I might seem to be debarred, as I have only one predecessor, and he, fortunately for us, is still alive. But, before there was a chair of medieval history, medieval studies were directed and sustained by the Dixie Professors of Ecclesiastical History, all of them distinguished medievalists, and they were therefore in a sense my predecessors, certainly my teachers. Creighton enriched our literature with his *History of the Papacy from the Great Schism to the Reformation*, a work of learning on the grand scale. He was before my time, but of both Gwatkin and Whitney I can speak from personal acquaintance, and gratefully acknowledge what I learnt from them and their unfailing kindness. Gwatkin was an amazing person, whose academic achievements even legend failed to exaggerate; he set out to show how medieval history should be taught, and his brilliant lectures, despite physical defects of voice and vision, inspired many of his hearers with enthusiasm for the subject. His massive learning was spiced with caustic comments and incisive judgments; like another famous Cambridge medievalist he entered the medieval lists *armatus et linguatus* as a champion of truth. Whitney will best be remembered for the generosity with which he expended himself in the service of others; he gave freely from his vast stores of learning and his large library, preferring, as he often said, to help others to write history rather than to write it himself. Gwatkin and Whitney were associated together as the first editors of the *Cambridge Medieval History*, and from volume IV onwards, my predecessor, Professor Previté-Orton, and I were similarly associated; the harmony of our partnership of fourteen years in that laborious undertaking remains as an abiding memory. Whitney, looking back on his association with Gwatkin, described himself as "pupil disguised as a colleague", and I can find no better phrase to express my indebtedness to my fellow-editor. I shall not attempt to emulate what he has already done so admirably in his Inaugural Lecture, in which he displayed the rich content of medieval history and revealed the interest and charm that are to be found therein. I am concerned with a more prosaic task. I propose to go round the department that is under my charge, like a manager of an industrial concern investigating whether the staff is adequate, whether there is a demand for the products of his firm, whether the machinery is up to date and the output of the right quality. It is on this humdrum tour of inspection that I invite you to accompany me, and to listen to my bald report, which will be mainly concerned with what I find amiss, what needs to be set right before the whole can function satisfactorily.

First of all, the domestic position. It is natural that a new Professor should make it his first care to take stock of the resources of the University and the Colleges for the teaching of his subject, and to investigate how the study of it progresses among the undergraduates; the promotion of post-graduate research is also his especial concern, both to guarantee the advancement of learning and to ensure the existence of a body of young graduates from whom future teachers can be recruited. I have had some months to ponder on these matters, and I have found this stock-taking a more depressing business than I had anticipated. In no respect is the position satisfactory. Medieval studies are not flourishing as they should in Cambridge; and this University is not making a contribution to them that is worthy of its fame or its traditions. Holding that opinion, I am bound to consider why this is so, and to analyse the causes. There is need for frankness here, and frankness is possible about a situation which has come about, as I think, quite unintentionally.

In the first place, the supply of teachers is inadequate. In 1939, of the twenty-nine Faculty and Assistant Faculty Lecturers only eight were medievalists. Since then two lecturers, B. L. Manning and J. G. Sykes, have died, and both of them were medievalists. There have been one or two other changes, but if all those who are now absent return to Cambridge, we shall resume after the war with twenty-five Lecturers and Assistant Lecturers; of these only four will be medievalists. Equally important with the provision of lecturers by the University is the provision made by the Colleges for supervision. Only a minority of Colleges have a medievalist on their teaching staff, and the proportion of modern historians to medieval among supervisors is at least four to one. This is perhaps more serious than the shortage of lecturers, since supervisors play such an important part in directing the work of undergraduates and maintaining their interest.

Possibly the gaps caused by death or promotion will be filled up, and the number of medieval lecturers raised to its pre-war level. I hope for something more than that, but then the question of recruitment obtrudes itself. For some years the training of students in the literary faculties has been interrupted, and it will be long before this can be made good. And even before the war the number of students engaged in medieval research was small, very small if we exclude Ph.D. candidates who came from outside and consider only our own graduates. This is not surprising when we note that an almost insignificant fraction of those who took Part II of the Tripos in those years chose a medieval special period.

Here then we have something that cannot be gainsaid, disconcerting as it is to the medievalist: very few third-year students are willing to specialise in medieval history. What is the reason for this? When the present Tripos was debated in the Senate in 1934, one speaker asserted that, as hardly anyone took the medieval special periods in Part II, evidently the students had acquired in Part I a distaste for medieval history. Obvious as that conclusion sounds, it is, I am sure, incorrect; the evidence I have had from other supervisors and personally from men of various Colleges has convinced me that many of them find it anything but distasteful. The real causes lie much deeper, and are partly to be found in external circumstances, partly in the nature of our Tripos. It is not to be expected, nor indeed is it desirable, that medieval history should attract as many students as modern. Apart from their inclinations, they are also swayed by their choice of a career. Thus a medievalist is of little demand as a school teacher, since in the majority of schools modern history alone is taught; and for certain of the most prized posts in the Civil Service a knowledge of modern history is essential.

There is one factor that militates against medieval specialisation, which has already been stressed by Professor Whitney. "I can speak", he says, "of experience gained in fixing special subjects for various examinations: at Cambridge, in London, and in Canada, we were hampered by the lack of suitable texts, and in consequence some periods and subjects had to reappear with a frequency they did not deserve.... There are few modern English texts properly edited." To this I might add that most of these English texts are out of print and extremely expensive. Many interesting periods, which would be attractive to students, especially in English history, cannot be set. We badly need a series of cheap texts for students.

Then there is the difficulty of language. The majority of men will always look for a special period which does not necessitate knowledge of a foreign language, and one of the modern periods almost always meets this requirement, while none of them requires anything more formidable than French. But those who wish to take a medieval special period may sometimes have to face authorities in Italian or medieval French, and will always have to face authorities in Latin. There was a time, within my own memory, when Latin was the basis of all literary education. Now it is adequately taught only to the dwindling band of classical specialists; for others it suffices that they should be able to satisfy the minimum requirements of the School Certificate Examination. From history scholars we expect a somewhat higher standard, but not enough to enable them to read Latin with any ease. There is, moreover, an unreasoning dread of medieval Latin, which the study of Stubbs's Charters does nothing to allay; but, after all, legal jargon is always terrifying to the layman. Really it is classical purists who have done most to instil this awe of the unknown. In their scorn of a Latinity so different from that of the Augustan age, they have treated it as a debased language written by men ignorant of the pure well of Latin undefiled. This is most ungrateful of them, for it is to the zeal of medieval scholars that they themselves owe all their knowledge of classical Latin; no manuscript of a Latin author written prior to the Middle Ages exists. The long lists of Latin authors in monastic and cathedral libraries testify to the knowledge and enthusiasm of medieval scribes, and it was these medieval manuscripts that made possible the revival of classical learning in the age of the Renaissance. There were some zealots in earlier times like Pope Gregory the Great

8

who "despised the cases which followed prepositions and refused to bind the oracles of God under the rules of the grammarian Donatus", but later scribes saw to it that the writings of the saintly Pope were not marred by grammatical blunders. In fact, most writers were careful to keep the rules of Latin grammar, in which they had been as thoroughly grounded as any of their modern traducers. The sneer about "monkish Latin" will continue to be made by people who have never read a line of a monastic chronicler; but it was invented by men who had read and even presumed to edit them. As Professor Claude Jenkins says in his lecture on "The Monastic Chronicler": "The writers of the Middle Ages, like those of the New Testament scriptures, have often suffered a little in the past from being edited by scholars who regarded them as careless if not ignorant reproducers of a debased form of classical Latin or Greek instead of as writers of a living language." That is the point: it is not a dead but a living language, and naturally in the course of a thousand years many words changed their meaning or their use and a large number of new words were introduced. When once the strangeness of the vocabulary has been mastered, it will be found that medieval writers are easier to read than their classical predecessors; it is only when unknown that they are frightening. The reluctant schoolboy who has struggled in the wake of Caesar through Gaul, or marched many weary parasangs before breakfast with Xenophon, might be aroused to interest if he could read instead some pages of the history of his native land in, say, the Venerable Bede,

9

William of Malmesbury, or Matthew Paris; and he would find them no harder to construe.

So far I have been dealing with obstacles to medieval research that are of general application. When we look at historical output as a whole in this country, we do not find that the medieval, either in quantity or quality, falls very far short of the modern. In learned articles, in the *English Historical Review* and elsewhere, it stands almost on an equality. Medieval history certainly appears to have special attractions of its own to counterbalance the difficulties its students have to face. So there must be special circumstances within our own curriculum that make it less attractive here than elsewhere. The great preponderance of modern historians on our teaching staffs may be one such circumstance; another that there is often only one special period available for medievalists, and that, as I have said, may not be sufficiently interesting except to a few. But the most important reason of all is to be found in the structure of our Tripos. Part II is so designed that, except for the ancient and medieval special periods, all the subjects are modern; candidates who wish to choose a medieval period find that it is out of keeping with the rest of their work, and therefore often change their mind. I have known a number of cases, and here again I have the evidence of other supervisors to support my own, of students interested in medieval history, anxious to pursue it further, but deterred by the curriculum of Part II. In order to have a course of study in which the subjects were reasonably co-ordinated and to some extent inter-related, they were compelled, however reluctantly, to select a modern special period. I am sure that the way in which our Tripos is constructed does operate most strongly to the disadvantage of medieval studies, indirectly as it affects the subsequent teaching, directly as it deters students from medieval specialisation. The Historical Tripos, as I first knew it, was somewhat differently organised. Special periods were compulsory in Part I, so that it was possible to work on a medieval special period in a general setting of medieval subjects; there was a regular choice of medieval periods, and perhaps Latin was not then so unfamiliar a language. In these conditions quite a number of candidates chose a medieval period. This system was changed in 1910, when special periods were relegated to Part II: their rightful place, I agree, but they were then put in an environment of modern subjects only. From that time, while the number of historical students has steadily increased, the number taking a medieval special period has as steadily declined.

There are two considerations to set off against the rather gloomy picture I have been painting. First, as far as encouragement to, and research in, medieval history is concerned, the women's Colleges are doing all or more than could be expected. When their share, out of all proportion to their numbers, is deducted, the deficiency in the men's Colleges becomes still more apparent. Secondly, the lack of numbers is offset by the enthusiasm of those who are teaching or researching. The habit of meeting together, of sharing knowledge, of general discussion, gave a stimulus to medieval studies in the period between the two wars which helped materially to keep them flowering under adverse conditions; here again the women played a disproportionate part. When normality returns and research again becomes possible, it is that healthy association that I shall be most anxious to see revived. Some of the obstacles to medieval study in this University are obviously remediable, and I know that I shall have support from my modern colleagues. My knowledge, too, of the enthusiasm of my medieval colleagues gives me every reason to be hopeful of the future, in which they will have a larger part to play than I.

The neglect of medieval history will not seem unfortunate to those people who believe that knowledge of the history of the past hundred years is all that is necessary to-day. Against this tendency our Regius Professor last term uttered a warning; and my predecessor in his Inaugural Lecture pointed to various directions in which a knowledge of the Middle Ages was required for the understanding of later events and ideas. I do not need here to make a detailed defence of medieval studies. But I should like to point out one or two ways in which a neglect of medieval history has been, to my mind, unfortunate. I was reminded of one by a sentence in a recent address by the Oxford Regius Professor: "From one point of view the Christian religion is a direct invitation to the study of history." If that invitation were generally accepted, there would be considerable demand for our services, for, from the nature of his subject, every medievalist must be in some degree an ecclesiastical historian. There is, however, little response to the invitation, even from the clergy, at any rate of the Church of England; and, to judge by the recent report of the Archbishops' Committee on the training of ordinands, their interest is not likely to be stimulated in the future.

Now I am bold enough to urge that even for modern diplomats a knowledge of medieval history would be of practical utility. That may seem a surprising statement, since only nineteenth- and twentieth-century history is considered necessary for their education. But to many peoples to-day, especially in Eastern Europe, their medieval history is much more of a reality than the immediate past. The Foreign Secretary, speaking in the House of Commons of the Poles, said that they were "too historically minded". This is a true indictment, but it follows that if you do not know their history you will be unable to understand their mind. It is natural for a country that has no modern history to wish to start again from its days of greatness, in the tenth century under Boleslav the Mighty, or still more in the later Middle Ages when in union with Lithuania they won the great victory at Tannenberg over the Teutonic knights in the north, and in the south were masters of the Ukraine and Kiev; here, of course, they conflict with the historical memory of the Russians, for Kiev was the beginning and the core of the Russian state. What is true of Poland is true of Bohemia, now known as Czechoslovakia, and of the various peoples included in the modern Jugoslavia. How precious to all these peoples is their medieval history Professor Previté-Orton and I had frequent occasion to realise when we edited the *Cambridge Medieval History*. Medieval history also provided a clue in the brief period of Republican Spain; the decentralising tendency was a direct reversion to the Middle Ages. The victory of the Falange resulted in the glorification of the fifteenth-century creators of Spanish unity—Ferdinand and Isabella—suitable models for a totalitarian ruler, for they instituted both a regime of autocracy and a purge of Spanish blood, resulting in the ruthless persecution of non-Spanish elements, Moors and especially Jews. The Jews themselves, the most cruelly treated of all peoples and therefore perhaps the most historically-minded, naturally look behind their medieval Diaspora, of which the Spanish persecutions were a belated epilogue, and concentrate on the greatness of their national life over 2000 years ago; and nobody blames them, for even modern politicians are acquainted with Old Testament history. But diplomats would do well also to make themselves acquainted with the history of Islam in the Middle Ages and the period of Arab greatness, even though it was a thousand or more years ago.

Other instances of the importance of the Middle Ages in modern times could be given—Italy and its divisions, created in the Middle Ages but still having their effect in a country only united in 1870; the great problem of Alsace-Lorraine; the German *Drang nach Osten*, beginning in the tenth century, continuous since the twelfth, and a cardinal factor in Nazi policy. The legend of the Herrenvolk also had to have its medieval origins, so the early history of Germany was falsified and rewritten. We have our greatness in modern times and are careless of our medieval past; other nations, less fortunate, ignore their modern history.

Well, I know that I am only beating the air. In the re-settlement of Europe historians will be consulted, as they were at Versailles, but only historians of recent events. Our claims to be consulted will be rebuffed, as those of the Commons were by James I: "do not meddle with the main points of government; that is my craft; *tractent fabrilia fabri*". So I return humbly to my own craft, and there is enough to keep me employed. Far too much to mention here. I must confine my survey to English history, and to that part of it which most needs attention: there are many defects in the foundations, and many of our tools need refurbishing.

In the workshops of history many types of craftsman are engaged, and each has his part in the finished article. It is none of it mechanical labour, and it needs apprenticeship. The experts in palaeography and diplomatic, in the science of language, in archaeology, help to lay the foundations and construct the materials; the geographer, the anthropologist, the psychologist all have their share in the main structure; and as it rises form is given to its parts by other technicians, trained in legal and administrative, economic and social, religious and philosophical, methods and ideas. The historical architect, though he need not be an expert in these crafts, must be familiar in some degree with the technique of many of them. He must have served his apprenticeship; otherwise he can never know whether the material he is using is the right material, or the use to which he is putting it is the right use. We need not worry about the old discussion whether history is a science or an art. For no true craftsman can adhere to the one at the expense of the other; an historical as any other edifice should be both functional and beautiful; a rigid technique, integrity of mind, and artistic sense are as necessary to the historian as they are to the architect and the artist. The writing of history, therefore, is the job of the trained, that is to say the professional craftsman. But it has often been usurped by the amateur and the dilettante, who have not served their apprenticeship: not appreciating the functional meaning of the parts, they build up a façade which is structurally unsound; not understanding the nature of their materials, they are little better than jerry builders. At the present time modern history would seem to be more affected than medieval by this invasion, but in the long run I think medieval history has suffered most; it has been hit in a more vital part, for the untrained amateur has taken a hand in the construction of its materials. As a nation we are prone to worship the amateur and rather to look down our noses at the professional, but I hope that as historians we shall not be too anxious to preserve our amateur status, even though we are often not paid for our labours.

Not every historical craftsman is engaged in the final stages. The antiquary and the editor of texts, for instance, prepare the material on which others can work, and their task is often for them an end in itself. There is the thrill of discovery, the ardour of the collector to inspire them and, if they have perfected their technique and maintained the integrity of their craftsmanship, they are making the task of other workers lighter and playing a vital part in the whole structure. But it is just because so much of this work has been done by untrained amateurs that what should be an aid is often a handicap to the medieval historian. For other reasons, too, there are many obstacles in the way of medieval research, and a great deal of re-organisation is needed to improve the study in its initial stages.

We start with manuscripts, the ultimate source of all our knowledge, and the first desideratum is that they should be readily accessible to the student. There is an initial difficulty in this country, owing to the circumstances attending the dissolution of the monasteries, that manu-scripts have been widely dispersed throughout the land; the number and variety of their owners is bewildering. The majority are in public or institutional libraries, themselves very numerous, and are accessible to the student, though in a few cases corporate bodies are not curious about their treasures or anxious that others should be; many are in private hands, and are not always easy of access, while it is often impossible to trace those that have passed through the auction room from one private owner to another. Many English manuscripts are in foreign libraries; in other countries manuscripts are not so widely dispersed as in England, but they are sometimes more difficult of access.

Secondly, the contents of these numerous libraries should be made known in printed catalogues. Cataloguing of manuscripts is a specialised task, needing the co-operation of several experts. The collections even in the greater libraries, here and abroad, are often most inadequately catalogued—the great Cotton collection in the British Museum is a case in point. Moreover, few institutions have troubled to publish a list of their archives, or private individuals of the manuscripts in their possession. Fortunately in 1869 the Historical MSS. Commission was appointed to inquire into both these sources of historical information in England, and its numerous reports have gone a long way towards filling what was a serious gap in our knowledge; but of course the Commission cannot guarantee that the manuscripts reported on are still *in situ*.

The third stage is to co-ordinate all this heterogeneous material that is stored in libraries at home and abroad. This needs a carefully planned concerted effort, and so far only one attempt has been made, and that by a single individual, Sir Thomas Duffus Hardy, for the chronicle and biographical sources of our medieval history. In the years 1862–1871 he published in three volumes in the Rolls Series his *Descriptive Catalogue of Materials relating to the History of Great Britain and Ireland to the end of the reign of Henry VII*. This has proved invaluable as a starting point for many scholars, and was truly an heroic undertaking. It was never completed, for he actually got no further than the death of Edward II (1327). And the enterprise was really beyond the powers of a single individual; it was bound to be incomplete, even for English manuscripts, still more for those in foreign libraries, with which Hardy had little acquaintance. The passage of time and recent discoveries have tended to lessen its usefulness; for instance, whereas Hardy in 1871 only knew of thirteen manuscripts containing letters of Robert Grosseteste, Professor S. H. Thompson in 1940 was able to list forty-one, thirty-three of them in English libraries. Hardy, while taking a justifiable pride in his achievement, was the first to recognise its imperfections, and in a wise and most instructive preface to his first volume he pointed out the path to perfection. After pleading for a MSS. Commission such as was actually established seven years later, he described how the Governments of France and Germany had employed scholars to travel abroad and to collect from foreign libraries material for the history of their own countries. Thus the foundations of the great *Monumenta Germaniae Historica* were laid by the journeys of Pertz, Waitz and others, and the large collections of material they were able to accumulate. Hardy urged that the Government of this country should employ scholars in the same way, but apart from Round's excellent *Calendar of Documents preserved in France* and the somewhat unsatisfactory *Calendar of entries in the papal registers relating to Great Britain and Ireland*, nothing has been done. Both of these deal with rather specialised types of material, and cover only a limited period: the former ends at 1200, the latter begins in 1198; and the value of both series was limited by the conditions imposed on the editors. Finally, Hardy was most anxious that his work should be kept up to date. "Subsequent investigators", he says, "will doubtless be able to correct and expand what has been here attempted. Interleaved copies of these volumes will, therefore, be deposited in the Public Libraries of Cambridge, Oxford, and Dublin, in the British Museum, and in the Public Library at Edinburgh, in order that any new materials that may be collected shall be available for a second edition." That was written over eighty years ago; there never has been a second edition. I do not know whether his plan of interleaved copies was carried into execution; certainly no trace of one can be found in our own Library. So it remains necessary for every individual if he wishes to make his work complete, to ransack for himself every English and continental library. Few can spare the time, or afford the expense; in any case, what a wasteful reduplication of effort!

The next stage, after collection and classification of the material, would be to make accessible in print as many historical sources as possible. In the case of certain classes of documents a brief précis may be sufficient, but at any rate for narrative sources the full text is obviously essential. This could only be done on a large scale at public expense, and the Government rendered a great service to historical learning when, after various false starts, it inaugurated in 1858 the publication of the *Chronicles and Memorials of Great Britain and Ireland during the Middle Ages*, known as the Rolls Series, because it was produced (*more Britannico*) under the direction of the Master of the Rolls. But this great series suffers from various defects. It was started before Hardy's *Descriptive Catalogue* had given a preliminary survey of the manuscripts of the various chronicles. The classically trained Government officials bound the editors by regulations suitable perhaps for the editing of classical texts, but most unsatisfactory for the editing of historical sources. Finally, their choice of editors, made on much the same principles, was often unfortunate. On the one hand, we rejoice in the splendid volumes edited by Stubbs, whose introductions were in themselves notable contributions to medieval history; on the other, we lament that a number of important works were entrusted to gentlemen without the necessary palaeographical or historical training, and moreover, as Professor Jenkins says in the passage I have already quoted, prejudiced against their authors because of the character of their Latinity. The series then, valuable as it is, is most unequal in quality, and a number of the volumes badly need re-editing. Moreover, before the end of the nineteenth century, an abrupt end was made to the editing of these primary sources, so that the series is far from complete. Among the most valuable sources for the history of the eleventh and twelfth centuries are the remarkable collections of letters of leading men of the time. Most of these had already been printed by that indefatigable but quite incompetent editor, J. A. Giles, and in time for them to be reproduced, with many additional blunders, in the *Patrologia* of the abbé Migne. The zeal of Canon Robertson salvaged all that could be termed *Materials for the history of Archbishop Thomas Becket* and published them in three volumes of the Rolls Series; and the letters of bishop Arnulf of Lisieux have recently been edited by Dr Barlow for the Royal Historical Society. But, for the important correspondence of archbishop Lanfranc, Gilbert Foliot, John of Salisbury, we are still at the mercy of Giles's editions. For the large and important collection of St Anselm's letters we have no edition more recent than the seventeenth-century one by Gerberon. So, what should have been a monument, as it was in Germany, remains in England a torso, with some of its completed features beautifully delineated, others roughly and clumsily executed. Here again may I repeat that what medieval students at all stages most need is a series of cheap, well-edited texts, such as exists in France and Germany.

For charters and records the position is certainly better, though many of the old collections, Wilkins's *Concilia* and Dugdale's *Monasticon* for instance, badly need re-editing. Calendars of State Papers are still being produced at public expense, and here again Duffus Hardy was a pioneer. Numerous private societies have been formed, some of which have fallen by the way owing to lack of financial support, to edit in full documents of particular kinds. The work done, for instance, by the Pipe Roll Society and the Selden Society needs no eulogy from me. The Royal Historical Society, too, publishes in its Camden Series material of all kinds. And in all these the standard of editing has improved out of all knowledge; the amateur editor has been eliminated and trained scholars employed. To these must be added the valuable publications of local societies, usually concerned with the records of a county, which are almost bewildering in their number and sometimes, too, in the peculiarity of their titles. To those that were in existence before 1915 Gross in his *Sources and Literature of English History to about* 1485, as to so much else, provides a key; but even he failed to detect the only publication which is devoted to the antiquities of the county of Hereford: it is known as the *Transactions of the Woolhope Naturalists' Field Club*. We need some guide through the maze of periodical literature.

Finally, in this survey of initial difficulties I must mention the need for more and better works of reference; for instance, dated lists of men of greater or lesser importance on which we could rely and which editors of texts and documents could employ without misgiving. Grateful as we are for the many learned articles in the *Dictionary of National Biography*, what a boon it would be if a comprehensive work on the scale of *Who's Who* could be compiled for the medieval period. Working in that most fascinating century of the English Middle Ages—the twelfth—I feel the need particularly. I have spoken already of the great epistolary collections of this period; they can only be dated and arranged when we know more about the persons mentioned in them. The numerous charters, public and private, which if collected would throw considerable light on legal, political, and social conditions, can also only be dated by means of our knowledge of the persons mentioned in them or the witnesses who attest them. If we work from the known to the unknown a great deal can be done. In one class of documents—papal bulls—

the date is often given or can very narrowly be determined. There are a large number of papal bulls, originals or in transcript, in English libraries, and those prior to 1200 have recently been edited, though it was left to a German, Professor Holtzmann, to do this and only two of his three volumes have appeared in print. Apart from their general value for ecclesiastical history, they help us to date numerous ecclesiastics, and in some cases supply us with the names, especially of heads of monastic houses, unknown before. I believe that from printed sources alone a fairly complete list could be compiled of all cathedral dignitaries and heads of monastic houses, and could be closely dated in many cases, and probably, though I cannot speak with the same confidence or knowledge, lists of the more important laymen as well. Such works of reference would be invaluable, and would save editors and researchers many hours of tedious and unnecessary search. Towards this, what have we at present? The episcopal lists, so admirably compiled by Stubbs, and repeated in the *Handbook of British Chronology*, published by the Royal Historical Society, which also gives lists of ministers of state and peers; for important laymen there is a good deal of information in various genealogical publications which needs collecting. For cathedral dignitaries other than bishops we have only Le Neve's *Fasti Ecclesiae Anglicanae*, published in 1716 and re-edited by Duffus Hardy in 1854. I have already had occasion to express the debt historians owe to Hardy, but I cannot say the same in this instance. For the twelfth and most of the thirteenth century his edition contains more names than the original, but at the same time far more blunders. It is not only useless, it is positively dangerous to employ it as a work of reference, and I could quote a number of mistakes made by modern editors who too trustingly relied on its names and dates. Almost equally worthless are the lists of heads of monastic houses given in the latest edition of Dugdale's *Monasticon*, and the volumes of the *Victoria County History* are, with a few notable exceptions, little more reliable. Many of the errors in all these works were due, I believe, to an excessive reliance on that most untrustworthy of eighteenth-century antiquaries, Browne Willis. But, having said that, let me hasten to add that in general I have nothing but admiration for that long line of antiquaries, stretching from Leland in the sixteenth century to the present day, who have devoted their lives to discovering, collecting, preserving the records of our medieval past. In earlier times they were often hasty, sometimes very careless, usually opinionated, but their achievement is much more remarkable than their faults, and they deserve our deep gratitude for what through their enthusiasm has been preserved to us. We are the heirs of their labours, and the fault is ours if we are content to live on our legacy, and do not rather make it the basis of a richer legacy to be handed on to our successors.

With the close of the eighteenth century a new era began, in which the great figures were historians rather than antiquaries. They too have left us a legacy for which we are often insufficiently grateful. How many people have been incited to the study of history by reading Gibbon (and

Macaulay), and how many might still be attracted to the Middle Ages if Gibbon was read to-day. The best approach to history is still, I believe, to start with the great masters; in detail they may be out of date, but their inspiration remains. Of course it was history with a bias, often with a purpose, into which modern party politics could enter, as in the rival Greek histories of Thirlwall and Grote. It was also an age of scientific discovery, and the lessons of science soon began to take effect. They have been of immense value as a means, in training the historical craftsman in his technique, but of some danger when regarded as an end, lest who should be a craftsman becomes a machine. We have been buffeted between the rival claims of the impersonal and the all-too-personal. Perhaps it is from the latter that medieval history has suffered most. For the Middle Ages became a battleground of a new War of Religion—to some it was an enlightened Age of Faith, to others a dark Age of Superstition and Ignorance—and Dogma claimed the right to state what were or were not historical facts. Nor was that all, for the Romantics staked their claim for the Age of Chivalry. We have weathered the storm now, but the waves have not quite died down and it is not always possible to avoid the spray.

However, the general historical conscience has improved enormously of recent years, and at the same time there has been a considerable advance in technique. I have spoken of the unscholarly nature of many of the editions and works of reference on which we have to depend. What a world of difference there is between the *Fasti* of Le Neve and the

Registrum Sacrum Anglicanum of Stubbs. Compare the charters of Salisbury or of Gloucester edited in the Rolls Series or of Hereford in the Cantilupe Society with the recent editions of the charters of York and Lincoln, and it is manifest what an advance in scholarship has come about. There are various reasons for this, but I only want to dwell for a moment on those who, by example or precept, have particularly helped to bring about this amelioration. We have had our great exemplars—I need only instance Stubbs and Maitland; we cannot perhaps attain to the standards they set, but we should be ashamed to accept lower ones. We have had our schoolmasters, too. One such, of the old-fashioned type, was that fine scholar, J. H. Round, who was ever on the watch, birch in hand, for blunders and ill-founded statements in historical exercises, and who frightened the slovenly into carefulness. His attack, a little too fierce perhaps, on Freeman is well known, and received a wider currency because it attracted the impish attention of Lytton Strachey, who was delighted at the denouncer of Froude being himself denounced for inaccuracy; yet he too sacrificed accuracy for effect when he described Round as "an obscure technician", "a burrower into wormholes, living in Brighton". Round was not a mere critic; he also set a high example. He put the science of genealogy on a new basis—with the result that very few people now can claim that their ancestors came over with the Conqueror. Also the Pipe Roll Society was extremely fortunate in having him as its editor, as it has been equally fortunate in his successors. Another, but an entirely different type of schoolmaster, was R. L. Poole, a meticulous scholar, mathematical almost in the neatness and precision of his conclusions. No one had more experience than he in the correction of historical exercises; he was a strict, but never a harsh, teacher. I should like to pay my personal tribute to him as teacher and friend from the time that I first, thirty-three years ago, had an article accepted by him. How many historical students learnt the finer points of their craft from him during the years that he edited the *English Historical Review*; and that journal, with its succession of distinguished editors, has played a notable part in the training of historians, medieval even more than modern.

I have chosen for mention only one or two names, out of a long list of those who helped to train the medieval apprentice, who have turned amateurs into professional craftsmen. And all the time I have been dealing with the early stages of our work; for in those early stages there is a lack of proper organisation, the tools are often faulty, the materials not up to specification, and before those defects are put right work in the later stages is seriously hampered. Also the problems that face the historical student afterwards are common to all historians, and I am concerned here with what is peculiar to the medievalist. Yet one problem—that of environment—is of more difficulty to him than to the modern or even to the ancient historian. It needs a greater effort to put oneself into the mind of a medieval man than of an Athenian or a Roman. It is a younger civilisation with more primitive, more child-like ideas. That is one of its fascinations, and it makes a great call on the historical imagination, without which interpretation of its events is impossible. But imagination can only function when it is fully acquainted with all the peculiar circumstances of the environment, and here we look for help to those who specialise in certain branches of our study—law, institutions and administration, economic and social life, intellectual and artistic endeavour. These experts naturally tend to be engrossed in the minutiae of their subject: by articles in learned journals or monographs on technical subjects they are adding to, or making repairs in, their part of the structure. To the non-expert, who cannot fit all these pieces, old and new, together so as to form a pattern, the whole has something of the appearance of a jig-saw puzzle. I want to plead with these experts in the various branches to co-ordinate for us the results of all their work; that is to say, that there should be a stock-taking at regular intervals, a synthesis of his subject by an expert in the light of the latest research. The objection raised to this is that the time is not ripe for such a synthesis; advance is rapid in certain directions, let us wait till things are more settled and we can get a clearer perspective of the whole. Surely the subject will always be in a fluid state, always advancing; when will the time be ripe? Naturally the expert prefers to write at first-hand on his own theme and not to summarise the conclusions of others; also, like Thucydides, he wishes to compose a κτῆμα ἐς ἀεί and we are asking from him what appears rather an ephemeral tour de force. If not ephemeral it will certainly eventually be out of date; such a synthesis needs to be revised at regular intervals. We cannot read all the articles and monographs; we cannot even keep stock of them all. For the undergraduate it is still more important; he cannot be fed entirely on monographs, nor can lectures supply the place of books. I know, from practical experience, that to write such a synthesis is a laborious, unsatisfying, humbling task; fellow experts will have plenty of faults to find; but it is not altogether a thankless task.

There are two other things for which I wish to plead with these specialists, though I do so with great diffidence and in the consciousness of my own imperfections. First, that the human element should be given a more prominent place. We do not know enough about the men of the Middle Ages; even for the greatest of them there are hardly any first-class biographies. The tendency is to concentrate on institutions and movements; but movements and institutions were made for man, not vice versa, and in the Middle Ages so much depends on the leading characters. Secondly, that in their writings they will be mindful of readers other than their fellow experts, so that the value and interest of their discoveries are not obscured by technicalities or overwhelmed by statistics. A historian, indeed, need not be afraid to display the processes of his mind, and to show the stages by which he arrived at his conclusions; the narration of an historical discovery may be as exciting as a detective story, if the language in which it is clothed be not too austere. Self revelation, however, should not be carried to extremes, as is the case sometimes in a Ph.D.

thesis where all the machinery is exposed naked to the view, so that the meaning is subordinated to the matter. Legal historians have the perfect model in Maitland, and medieval economic historians could pay no better tribute to the memory of Eileen Power than to imitate the charm and human feeling with which she invested her learning. And for social history the Master of Trinity has just done delightfully all those things for which I have been pleading, though, unfortunately for us, he only started with the later Middle Ages.

Finally, I want to say something on the relation of these parts to the whole. The essential unity of history is broken when we divide it vertically into isolated periods, or horizontally into isolated subjects. Too much have we in this University tended to keep these periods and subjects in separate compartments. It was intended in the present Tripos to make a whole of English history, and to avoid the old separation into political, economic and constitutional. But we arranged for the teachers to continue on the old lines, and left it to the students to dovetail the parts together, and so it was a failure. It is clear now that the synthesis, the really difficult thing, must be done, if at all, by the teachers. I hope that the experiment will be made again along different lines, and that a history of England will be our aim. That in itself will be only a part, though an important part to us, of the whole; but though the whole, the history of human civilisation, is too vast a subject for any one man to study, if it is seen as the whole, the period or subject we favour can rightly be fitted into its true place.

I am afraid there is a querulous tone throughout this lecture. It is usual on such occasions to dwell rather on the excellencies of one's subject than on the imperfections. But I am impressed by a sense of urgency which prevents me from being complacent. There is a great opportunity, with the prospect of a return to the pursuits of peace, to put one's house in order, and it is necessary to assess what has been done amiss in the past, so that we may make a fair start in the future. But my own period of authority is a brief one, and will have ended in four years' time. I feel that this is almost as much a valedictory as an inaugural lecture, and like Moses on Mt Pisgah I am given a sight of a promised land into which I shall not be able to enter. All the more need for me to dwell on the mistakes and difficulties of the past (I have some right to speak on this, as I have had a share in the teaching of medieval history in this University for more than thirty-five years), and thus constructively to prepare the way for a future of promise. As to the subject itself I have no misgivings. The history of the Middle Ages must always be an essential part of the history of mankind: it was a vital and a creative period, many of its works are among our most prized possessions, many of its thoughts are still bearing fruit to-day. It will never lack its interpreters; the workers in its fields do not admit drudgery in a task which arouses so much enthusiasm and gives so much delight; its difficulties and unfamiliarities will always be a spur and a challenge to the adventurous. What can I feel but pride in having a position of command in such an enterprise!

www.ingramcontent.com/pod-product-compliance
Ingram Content Group UK Ltd.
Pitfield, Milton Keynes, MK11 3LW, UK
UKHW042327020325
455765UK00001B/1